This book is for my mother,
with love and gratitude

Frances Lincoln Limited
4 Torriano Mews
Torriano Avenue
London NW5 2RZ

Copyright © Frances Lincoln Limited 2000
Introduction and commentary text copyright © Simon Callow 2000
For photographic acknowledgments and copyright details, see pages 120–125

British Library Cataloguing-in-Publication data

A catalogue record for this book is available from the British Library

ISBN 0 7112 1535 9

Printed in Hong Kong

9 8 7 6 5 4 3 2

Title page:
Detail of 'Ideal' portrait of William Shakespeare by Angelica Kauffman (from the RSC Collection with the permission of the Governors of the Royal Shakespeare Theatre, Stratford-upon-Avon)

Shakespeare on Love

A Personal Selection by
SIMON CALLOW

FRANCES LINCOLN

CONTENTS

INTRODUCTION

The novelist L.P. Hartley's famous remark about the past being another country is a great truth, but some pasts are stranger, more distant than others. Chaucer's characters are vivid enough, to be sure, but their patterns of thought are not like ours. It is not much of an exaggeration to say that Shakespeare's characters are the first in world literature whom we recognize as being like us: it is almost impossible to see or read one of his plays without exclaiming: 'I know someone exactly like that!' or, even more often, 'I have done that, felt that, thought that. I have been there.' His characters' behaviour has become for us the norm of all human behaviour. He got in first, leaving a map of the human soul which has influenced everyone who has written about it since.

Moreover, Shakespeare wrote from a position of identification. There is little sense in Shakespeare's plays of the author's personality; rather, each character seems to have a life entirely of his or her own, which means that the writer's range of sympathy must have been of an almost inconceivable breadth. To have inside you Romeo and Juliet, Othello and Desdemona, Cordelia and Regan, Caliban and Miranda must be uncomfortable, to say the least, and betokens a temperament so all-inclusive that it must have come perilously close to falling apart at the seams – an experience about which, of course, Shakespeare wrote with harrowing realism in more than one play.

Not only do his characters behave in ways which we recognize, they provoke considerable sympathy in us. Even those who are quite irredeem-

ably and unrepentantly evil – Iago, Richard Crookback – have a degree of life in them which makes them dangerously attractive, just as in life. Unlike his great contemporary, Ben Jonson, who was quite as sharp in his observation but full of cold fury towards the weakness of his fellow creatures, Shakespeare appears not to judge his characters, nor does he invite our judgment on them: that's life, he seems to say, in all its splendour and terror; this is what it is to be human. He is no moralist.

Nowhere does he more completely and sympathetically engage with the human experience than when he writes of love, which he does a great, great deal, almost compulsively, one might say. Of the thirty-seven plays contained in the First Folio of 1623, the following devolve centrally on love: *Antony and Cleopatra, The Comedy of Errors, Love's Labour's Lost, A Midsummer Night's Dream, Much Ado About Nothing, Othello, Romeo and Juliet, The Taming of the Shrew, Troilus and Cressida, Twelfth Night* and *The Two Gentlemen of Verona* – nearly a third of Shakespeare's entire output (the lost play *Love's Labour's Won* speaks for itself, and *Cardenio*, to which Shakespeare seems to have contributed, is another intensely love-drenched piece). In addition, the long poems *Venus and Adonis, A Lover's Complaint* and *The Rape of Lucrece* all concern love in one form or another, as well as the poems attributed to him in the collection *The Passionate Pilgrim*. As if this were not enough, the collection of Sonnets first published in 1609 amounts to what is perhaps the most sustained and intense record ever written of the devastating effects of, in this case, more than one relationship.

This brings us a little closer, perhaps, to the perennial question of who the extraordinary man was who wrote these plays (by which I mean what was William Shakespeare really like, not did he actually write the plays, which is a question unworthy of consideration), and offers some concrete

evidence with which to answer the titillating question of what kind of lover the man was who wrote so copiously and gloriously about love. Do the Sonnets really show us Shakespeare in love? If they do, the picture is a gloomy one. Love proves a largely unhappy experience for him: briefly enchanted, then obsessed, by the object of his love, an aristocratic young man, he soon feels himself to be old, mortal, ugly, socially inferior, unable to compete with his rivals, aching for love but insistent that he is unworthy of it, now begging to be ignored, next asking for his name never to be mentioned for fear of causing offence. In parallel with this probably non-sexual passion (but eventually interwoven with it) there is in the collection a group of sonnets which offer an account of an unmistakably carnal and consummated relationship with a mistress, equally full of conflicting emotions, though free of the romantic idealization the poet feels for the young man, and its consequent self-abasement. The culmination of the two relationships is, somehow inevitably, that the young man and the mistress sleep with each other: there is a strong suggestion that this has in some way been willed by the poet, who then attempts to repair the damage, being unprepared to lose either. Finally, though, he is simply unable to continue with the torment he undergoes, and bids the young man farewell; how he resolves things with his mistress is not revealed.

If we can assume that the 'I' of the Sonnets is Shakespeare himself (and there is no reason to believe that it is not), it is clear, on the strength of these poems, that Shakespeare's emotional life was as much of a mess as it is for most of us: but it is also clear that, unlike us, perhaps, he had no alternative. He was irresistibly compelled by love's imperatives: when love called, he could not refuse, and this it is that makes him such an inspired writer on the subject. 'Believe not,' says the Duke to the Friar in *Measure for Measure*, 'that the dribbling dart of love/Can pierce a complete bosom', but the message of Shakespeare's plays about love, and indeed all his writing on the subject, is that nobody's bosom is complete (even the Duke has fallen for Isabella by the end of the play) and that that dribbling dart will find you out wherever you are, for better or for worse.

In making the selection for this volume, I was struck by how widely the notion of love appears in Shakespeare's work, by no means solely confined to the amorous or the sexual sphere. I have accordingly appended a section which deals with other varieties of love: love of country, love of parents, love of children, even – for Shakespeare is not Britain's national poet for nothing – love of dog. (There is an even larger category which it would be truly impossible to include, for Shakespeare's love of life is simply boundless, and informs all these other loves. Only matrimonial love seems to have no place in his world view.) This book is, despite this final diversion, nonetheless substantially about the emotion that is responsible for the best and the worst experiences that most of us will have in this life, 'the heaven that leads men to this hell'. It remains astonishing that 400 years and more since the words in this volume were written, they continue to provide the freshest, most vital expression of it.

The last poem in the selection, a sonnet, is to some extent the key to the whole volume, celebrating, as it does, the way in which art can make love immortal. The poem promises that both the beloved and the love that the poet feels for him will not die: Shakespeare's art will guarantee that 'So long as men can breathe or eyes can see,/So long lives this, and this gives life to thee.' Truer word was never written: exactly as he predicted, we are still reading the poem, and the love that provoked it is as alive today as when he wrote it.

11

WHAT IS LOVE?

WHAT IS LOVE?

As You Like It is as complete an exploration of love as exists in
Shakespeare's output. The elaborate plot weaves three love stories together:
that of Orlando and Rosalind (who is disguised as a boy, Ganymede), Silvius
and Phoebe, and Audrey and Touchstone. In an extraordinary passage,
whose effect is almost as much musical as meaningful, four of the lovers try
to define the feeling that possesses them. With characteristic briskness,
Rosalind punctures the exalted atmosphere by saying: 'Pray you, no more of
this; 'tis like the howling of Irish wolves against the moon.' (Some howling;
some wolves.)

PHEBE	Good shepherd, tell this youth what 'tis to love.
SILVIUS	It is to be all made of sighs and tears; And so am I for Phebe.
PHEBE	And I for Ganymede.
ORLANDO	And I for Rosalind.
ROSALIND	And I for no woman.
SILVIUS	It is to be all made of faith and service, And so am I for Phebe.
PHEBE	And I for Ganymede.
ORLANDO	And I for Rosalind.
ROSALIND	And I for no woman.

SILVIUS   It is to be all made of fantasy,
All made of passion, and all made of wishes,
All adoration, duty, and observance,
All humbleness, all patience, and impatience,
All purity, all trial, all obedience;
And so am I for Phebe.

PHEBE   And so am I for Ganymede.

ORLANDO   And so am I for Rosalind.

ROSALIND   And so am I for no woman.

As You Like It, V.ii.

LOVE OF LOVE

Twelfth Night is another exquisite weaving of parallel and interlocking infatuations, again complicated by the need of one of the characters to wear the clothes of the opposite sex – in this case Viola, who has been ship-wrecked off the coast of Illyria. Orsino, Duke of Illyria, is hopelessly in love with a countess, Olivia, herself in deep mourning for her recently deceased brother. The play opens with Orsino in the grip of the delicious, capricious torments of love.

ORSINO   If music be the food of love, play on,
                 Give me excess of it, that, surfeiting,
                 The appetite may sicken and so die.
                 That strain again! It had a dying fall;
                 O, it came o'er my ear like the sweet sound
                 That breathes upon a bank of violets,
                 Stealing and giving odour! Enough, no more;
                 'Tis not so sweet now as it was before.
                 O spirit of love, how quick and fresh art thou!
                 That, notwithstanding thy capacity
                 Receiveth as the sea, nought enters there,
                 Of what validity and pitch soe'er,
                 But falls into abatement and low price
                 Even in a minute. So fall of shapes is fancy,
                 That it alone is high fantastical.

Twelfth Night; or, What You Will, I.i.

CALF LOVE

Romeo, young scion of the house of Montague, has also given himself up completely to love's seductions – but it is love itself that he is in love with rather than anyone in particular. That is still to come. The state of being in love is so similar to illness, or perhaps even madness, that his friend and family fear for him.

MONTAGUE   Many a morning hath he there been seen,
               With tears augmenting the fresh morning's dew,
               Adding to clouds more clouds with his deep sighs;
               But all so soon as the all-cheering sun
               Should in the farthest east begin to draw
               The shady curtains from Aurora's bed,
               Away from light steals home my heavy son,
               And private in his chamber pens himself,
               Shuts up his windows, locks fair daylight out,
               And makes himself an artificial night.
               Black and portentous must this humour prove,
               Unless good counsel may the cause remove.

BENVOLIO   My noble uncle, do you know the cause?

MONTAGUE   I neither know it nor can learn of him.

Romeo and Juliet, I.i.

18

FORBIDDEN LOVE

— 🌀 —

Prospero, the overthrown Duke of Milan, exiled to an exotic island, has by magic caused a storm which has shipwrecked the usurping duke, his brother, and all his court. Among them is Ferdinand, the son of the King of Naples. Prospero's daughter, Miranda, whom he has brought up with loving strictness, is astonished by her first sight of the young man: apart from her father she has never before set eyes on any mortal man. Ferdinand is equally enchanted by the sight of Miranda; but Prospero sets the young man to wood-cutting, to prove his worth. Miranda visits him at his work, unaware that they are being watched and judged by the old wizard.

FERDINAND   The very instant that I saw you, did
             My heart fly to your service; there resides
             To make me slave to it; and for your sake
             Am I this patient log-man.

MIRANDA   Do you love me?

FERDINAND   O heaven, O earth, bear witness to this sound,
             And crown what I profess with kind event,
             If I speak true! If hollowly, invert
             What best is boded me to mischief! I,
             Beyond all limit of what else i' th' world,
             Do love, prize, honour you.

MIRANDA   I am a fool
             To weep at what I am glad of.

PROSPERO   [*Aside*]   Fair encounter
             Of two most rare affections! Heavens rain grace
             On that which breeds between 'em!

                                        The Tempest, III.i.

LESSONS IN LOVE

*R*osalind, older and shrewder than Orlando, acquaints him with some blunt truths about love, testing the depth of his feeling for her. He, of course, has no idea that the strangely wise and confusingly attractive young man to whom he is speaking is Rosalind herself, in disguise.

ROSALIND	Love is merely a madness; and, I tell you, deserves as well a dark house and a whip as madmen do; and the reason why they are not so punish'd and cured is that the lunacy is so ordinary that the whippers are in love too. Yet I profess curing it by counsel.
ORLANDO	Did you ever cure any so?
ROSALIND	Yes, one; and in this manner. He was to imagine me his love, his mistress; and I set him every day to woo me; at which time would I, being but a moonish youth, grieve, be effeminate, changeable, longing and liking, proud, fantastical, apish, shallow, inconstant, full of tears, full of smiles; for every passion something and for no passion truly anything, as boys and women are for the most part cattle of this colour – would now like him, now loathe him; then entertain him, then forswear him; now weep for him, then spit at him; that I drave my suitor from his mad humour of love to a living humour of madness, which was, to forswear the full stream of the world and to live in a nook merely monastic. And thus I cur'd him . . .
ORLANDO	I would not be cured, youth.

As You Like It, III.ii.

LOVE IN THE SPRING

— ✿ —

The forest of Arden, to which Rosalind and her cousin Celia, following the recently banished Duke and his court, have escaped in disguise, is full of love and lovers of every shape, size, class and condition. Two of the Duke's pages celebrate the rising of the sap with the coming of spring.

2 PAGE   It was a lover and his lass,
　　　　　　　With a hey, and a ho, and a hey nonino,
　　　　　That o'er the green corn-field did pass
　　　　　　　In the spring time, the only pretty ring time,
　　　　　When birds do sing, hey ding a ding, ding.
　　　　　Sweet lovers love the spring.
　　　　　　　Between the acres of the rye,
　　　　　　　With a hey, and a ho, and a hey nonino,
　　　　　These pretty country folks would lie,
　　　　　　　In the spring time, the only pretty ring time,
　　　　　When birds do sing, hey ding a ding, ding.
　　　　　Sweet lovers love the spring.
　　　　　This carol they began that hour,
　　　　　　　With a hey, and a ho, and a hey nonino,
　　　　　How that a life was but a flower,
　　　　　　　In the spring time, the only pretty ring time,
　　　　　When birds do sing, hey ding a ding, ding.
　　　　　Sweet lovers love the spring.
　　　　　And therefore take the present time,
　　　　　　　With a hey, and a ho, and a hey nonino,
　　　　　For love is crowned with the prime,
　　　　　　　In the spring time, the only pretty ring time,
　　　　　When birds do sing, hey ding a ding, ding.
　　　　　Sweet lovers love the spring.

As You Like It, V.iii.

YOUNG LOVE

Feste, Olivia's jester, comments on the multiple couplings and intrigues taking place all around him. Here he sings of the urgency of love, striking at the end of his song the note of melancholy that is never far from lovers' thoughts: will love last?

FESTE   O mistress mine, where are you roaming?
                O, stay and hear; your true love's coming,
                  That can sing both high and low.
                  Trip no further, pretty sweeting;
                  Journeys end in lovers meeting,
                  Every wise man's son doth know . . .

                What is love? 'Tis not hereafter;
                Present mirth hath present laughter;
                  What's to come is still unsure.
                In delay there lies no plenty,
                Then come kiss me, sweet and twenty.
                  Youth's a stuff will not endure.

Twelfth Night; or, What You Will, II.iii.

Falling in Love

FIRST LOVE
ROMEO AND JULIET

LOVE'S RAPTURES
ROMEO AND JULIET

COMPLICATED LOVE
MUCH ADO ABOUT NOTHING

LOVE ACKNOWLEDGED
LOVE'S LABOUR'S LOST

BEWITCHED LOVE
A MIDSUMMER NIGHT'S DREAM

LOVE UNRECIPROCATED
AS YOU LIKE IT

LOVE FOR A YOUNGER MAN
VENUS AND ADONIS

FIRST LOVE

*R*omeo has directed his need to be in love on to the beautiful Rosaline, displaying all the classic symptoms of adolescent anguish. Then, gate-crashing a ball given by the family which is his family's deadly enemy, he sets eyes on Juliet, and imaginary love is replaced by the real thing. Immediately he starts to speak differently, and becomes, at a stroke, a poet instead of a mere versifier. After the ball he follows Juliet to her house and, with reckless passion, climbs over the perilously high garden wall to feast his eyes on her in the shadows.

ROMEO   But, soft what light through yonder window breaks?
                    It is the east, and Juliet is the sun.
                    Arise, fair sun, and kill the envious moon,
                    Who is already sick and pale with grief
                    That thou her maid art far more fair than she.
                    Be not her maid, since she is envious.
                    Her vestal livery is but sick and green,
                    And none but fools do wear it; cast it off.
                    It is my lady; O, it is my love!
                    O that she knew she were!
                    She speaks, yet she says nothing. What of that?
                    Her eye discourses; I will answer it.
                    I am too bold, 'tis not to me she speaks:
                    Two of the fairest stars in all the heaven,
                    Having some business, do entreat her eyes
                    To twinkle in their spheres till they return.
                    What if her eyes were there, they in her head?
                    The brightness of her cheek would shame those stars,
                    As daylight doth a lamp; her eyes in heaven
                    Would through the airy region stream so bright
                    That birds would sing, and think it were not night.
                    See how she leans her cheek upon her hand.
                    O that I were a glove upon that hand,
                    That I might touch that cheek!

Romeo and Juliet, II.ii.

LOVE'S RAPTURES

Juliet, on her balcony, is pondering the impossibility of her love for Romeo: if only he had another name! Romeo can hold his peace no more; he calls up to her; terrified for his safety, she answers him.

JULIET   How cam'st thou hither, tell me, and wherefore?
                The orchard walls are high and hard to climb,
                And the place death, considering who thou art,
                If any of my kinsmen find thee here.

ROMEO   With love's light wings did I o'er-perch these walls,
                For stony limits cannot hold love out,
                And what love can do, that dares love attempt.
                Therefore thy kinsmen are no stop to me.

JULIET   If they do see thee, they will murder thee.

ROMEO   Alack, there lies more peril in thine eye
                Than twenty of their swords; look thou but sweet,
                And I am proof against their enmity.

JULIET   I would not for the world they saw thee here.

ROMEO   I have night's cloak to hide me from their eyes;
                And but thou love me, let them find me here.
                My life were better ended by their hate
                Than death prorogued wanting of thy love.

Romeo and Juliet, II.ii.

COMPLICATED LOVE

*L*ove is by no means always straightforward, and is certainly not confined to the young and beautiful. Sometimes, too, it needs a helping hand. Benedick, a soldier in the army of Don Pedro, Prince of Arragon, is stationed in Messina, whose governor, Leonato, has a niece, Beatrice. There is 'a merry war' between Beatrice and Benedick, who delight in insulting each other. Don Pedro and his co-conspirators try to trick them into believing that each is really in love with the other. Eventually the miracle occurs, and the game becomes real.

BEATRICE   Against my will I am sent to bid you come in to dinner.

BENEDICK   Fair Beatrice, I thank you for your pains.

BEATRICE   I took no more pains for those thanks than you take pains to thank me; if it had been painful, I would not have come.

BENEDICK   You take pleasure, then, in the message?

BEATRICE   Yea, just so much as you may take upon a knife's point, and choke a daw withal. You have no stomach, signior; fare you well.   [*Exit.*

BENEDICK   Ha! 'Against my will I am sent to bid you come in to dinner' – there's a double meaning in that. 'I took no more pains for those thanks than you took pains to thank me' – that's as much as to say 'Any pains that I take for you is as easy as thanks.' If I do not take pity of her I am a villain. If I do not love her I am a Jew. I will go get her picture.

Much Ado About Nothing, II.iii.

LOVE ACKNOWLEDGED

The King of Navarre and his companions have repaired to his park to give themselves over, for a three-year span, to the scholarly life. Most important among the things that they determine to renounce is, of course, love; but their intentions are doomed, and one by one they succumb to the charms of the Princess of France and her ladies-in-waiting. The last to fall is Berowne, resident wit and cynic, given away by a more than usually soppy effusion in verse. Here he faces up to the truth: he is as susceptible as anyone else to love's power.

BEROWNE   And I forsooth, in love; I, that have been love's whip;
           A very beadle to a humorous sigh;
           A critic, nay, a night-watch constable;
           A domineering pedant o'er the boy,
           Than whom no mortal so magnificent!
           This wimpled, whining, purblind, wayward boy,
           This senior-junior, giant-dwarf, Dan Cupid;
           Regent of love-rhymes, lord of folded arms,
           Th' anointed sovereign of sighs and groans,
           Liege of all loiterers and malcontents,
           Dread prince of plackets, king of codpieces,
           Sole imperator, and great general
           Of trotting paritors. O my little heart!

Love's Labour's Lost, III.i.

Bewitched Love

The tempestuous relations between the immortals – Oberon, the King of
the Fairies, and his spouse, Titania – are mirrored by those in the human
world, where the couples Hermia and Lysander, Helena and Demetrius have
each fallen in love with the 'wrong' person in the eyes of their parents. They
flee to the forest to escape parental wrath, and become victims of Oberon's
mischief-making servant, Puck. A group of working men, rehearsing their
play in the forest (finding rehearsal space was a problem even in ancient
Athens), become involved in a plot to humiliate Titania when their noisiest
member, Bottom, is transformed into an ass, and Titania is drugged by Puck,
making her fall in love with Bottom in his beastly form. Here he has just
serenaded her.

TITANIA   I pray thee, gentle mortal, sing again.
Mine ear is much enamoured of thy note;
So is mine eye enthralled to thy shape;
And thy fair virtue's force perforce doth move me,
On the first view, to say, to swear, I love thee.

BOTTOM   Methinks, mistress, you should have little reason for that.
And yet, to say the truth, reason and love keep little company
together now-a-days. The more the pity that some honest
neighbours will not make them friends. Nay, I can gleek upon
occasion.

TITANIA   Thou art as wise as thou art beautiful.

BOTTOM   Not so, neither; but if I had wit enough to get out of this
wood, I have enough to serve mine own turn.

TITANIA   Out of this wood do not desire to go;
Thou shalt remain here whether thou wilt or no.
I am a spirit of no common rate;

The summer still doth tend upon my state;
And I do love thee; therefore go with me.
I'll give thee fairies to attend on thee;
And they shall fetch thee jewels from the deep,
And sing, while thou on pressed flowers dost sleep;
And I will purge thy mortal grossness so
That thou shalt like an airy spirit go.

A Midsummer Night's Dream, III.i.

LOVE UNRECIPROCATED

$\mathcal{D}$eep in the Forest of Arden, the shepherd Silvius is overwhelmed by his passion for Phebe, a shepherdess. She is cruelly indifferent to his eloquent effusions, having eyes only for the dashing young man calling himself Ganymede, but known to us as Rosalind.

PHEBE   Dead shepherd, now I find thy saw of might:
'Who ever lov'd that lov'd not at first sight?'

SILVIUS   Sweet Phebe.

PHEBE   Ha! What say'st thou, Silvius?

SILVIUS   Sweet Phebe, pity me.

PHEBE   Why, I am sorry for thee, gentle Silvius.

SILVIUS   Wherever sorrow is, relief would be.
If you do sorrow at my grief in love,
By giving love, your sorrow and my grief
Were both extermin'd.

PHEBE   Thou hast my love; is not that neighbourly?

SILVIUS   I would have you.

PHEBE   Why, that were covetousness.
Silvius, the time was that I hated thee;
And yet it is not that I bear thee love;
But since that thou canst talk of love so well,
Thy company, which erst was irksome to me,
I will endure; and I'll employ thee, too.
But do not look for further recompense
Than thine own gladness that thou art employ'd.

SILVIUS So holy and so perfect is my love,
And I in such a poverty of grace,
That I shall think it a most plenteous crop
To glean the broken ears after the man
That the main harvest reap; loose now and then
A scatt'red smile, and that I'll live upon.

As You Like It, III.v.

LOVE FOR A YOUNGER MAN

In Shakespeare's long poem *Venus and Adonis*, Venus, goddess of love, conceives a desperate passion for the coldly beautiful youth Adonis, who rejects her absolutely. Nothing she can say or do – and she goes to some lengths, both physically and verbally – will persuade him to love her. Finally, at the climax of a wild hunt, he is killed by a boar, leaving Venus to lament the loss of such flawless beauty. Here is a part of her earlier attempt at seduction.

'The tender spring upon thy tempting lip
Shows thee unripe; yet mayst thou well be tasted;
Make use of time, let not advantage slip;
Beauty within itself should not be wasted.
   Fair flowers that are not gath'red in their prime
   Rot and consume themselves in little time.

'Were I hard-favour'd, foul or wrinkled-old,
Ill-nurtur'd, crooked, churlish, harsh in voice,
O'er-worn, despised, rheumatic, and cold,
Thick-sighted, barren, lean, and lacking juice,
   Then mightst thou pause, for then I were not for thee;
   But having no defects, why dost abhor me?

'Thou canst not see one wrinkle in my brow;
Mine eyes are grey, and bright, and quick in turning;
My beauty as the spring doth yearly grow,
My flesh is soft and plump, my marrow burning;
   My smooth moist hand, were it with thy hand felt,
   Would in thy palm dissolve or seem to melt.

'Bid me discourse, I will enchant thy ear,
Or, like a fairy, trip upon the green,
Or, like a nymph, with long dishevelled hair,
Dance on the sands, and yet no footing seen.

Love is a spirit all compact of fire,
Not gross to sink, but light, and will aspire.'

Venus and Adonis

Love's Complications

BRUTAL LOVE
MEASURE FOR MEASURE

LOVE MOCKED
TWELFTH NIGHT

IMPATIENT LOVE
ROMEO AND JULIET

COURTSHIP
OTHELLO

FOLIE À DEUX
ANTONY AND CLEOPATRA

LOVE'S ECSTASY
SONNET LIII

LOVE DAY AND NIGHT
SONNET XLIII

ROYAL LOVE
KING HENRY THE FIFTH

BRUTAL LOVE

Vincentio, the wise and tolerant Duke of Vienna, has stepped aside in
favour of his deputy, Angelo, a man of fiercely puritanical cast. As one of the
first actions of his regime, Angelo condemns to death a young gentleman,
Claudio, for impregnating his girlfriend, Juliet. Claudio's pious sister,
Isabella, comes to Angelo to plead for his life. In the course of their
interview, Angelo is shaken to find himself overpowered by lust for her.

ISABELLA   . . . I'll tell the world aloud
            What man thou art.

ANGELO   Who will believe thee, Isabel?
            My unsoil'd name, th' austereness of my life,
            My vouch against you, and my place i' th' state,
            Will so your accusation overweigh
            That you shall stifle in your own report,
            And smell of calumny. I have begun,
            And now I give my sensual race the rein:
            Fit thy consent to my sharp appetite:
            Lay by all nicety and prolixious blushes
            That banish what they sue for; redeem thy brother
            By yielding up thy body to my will;
            Or else he must not only die the death,
            But thy unkindness shall draw his death draw out
            To ling'ring sufferance. Answer me to-morrow . . .

Measure for Measure, II.iv.

LOVE MOCKED

*O*livia, unresponsive object of Orsino's passion, is the mistress of a somewhat unruly household, which includes her kinsman Sir Toby Belch, his friend Sir Andrew Aguecheek, her jester, Feste, and their constant companion, Maria, Olivia's waiting woman. The bane of this merry group's life is Olivia's steward, Malvolio, a Puritan cross-patch, who dedicates his life to curtailing their pleasures. They plot their revenge: they will make him believe that Olivia is in love with him, writing him a note in her handwriting to that effect. They then hide behind the bushes and watch their jape work better than even they had imagined possible: he is utterly convinced.

MALVOLIO   Daylight and champain discovers not more. This is open. I will be proud, I will read politic authors, I will baffle Sir Toby, I will wash off gross acquaintance, I will be point-devise the very man. I do not now fool myself to let imagination jade me; for every reason excites to this, that my lady loves me. She did commend my yellow stockings of late, she did praise my leg being cross-garter'd; and in this she manifests herself to my love, and with a kind of injunction drives me to these habits of her liking. I thank my stars I am happy. I will be strange, stout, in yellow stockings, and cross-garter'd, even with the swiftness of putting on. Jove and my stars be praised! Here is yet a postscript.

     [*Reads*] 'Thou canst not choose but know who I am. If thou entertain'st my love, let it appear in thy smiling; thy smiles become thee well. Therefore in my presence still smile, dear my sweet, I prithee.'

Jove, I thank thee. I will smile; I will do everything that thou wilt have me.

Twelfth Night, or What You Will, II.v.

IMPATIENT LOVE

$\mathcal{R}$omeo and Juliet's mutual passion is such that they cannot delay its consummation for a moment. Friar Lawrence, Romeo's confessor, marries them secretly, after which Juliet returns home to wait with desperate impatience for the cloak of night to descend, under which Romeo can come to her.

JULIET   Gallop apace, you fiery-footed steeds
               Towards Phoebus' lodging; such a waggoner
               As Phaethon would whip you to the west,
               And bring in cloudy night immediately.
               Spread thy close curtain, love-performing night,
               That runaways' eyes may wink, and Romeo
               Leap to these arms, untalk'd of and unseen.
               Lovers can see to do their amorous rites
               By their own beauties; or if love be blind,
               It best agrees with night. Come, civil night,
               Thou sober-suited matron, all in black,
               And learn me how to lose a winning match,
               Play'd for a pair of stainless maidenhoods;
               Hood my unmann'd blood, bating in my cheeks,
               With thy black mantle, till strange love, grown bold,
               Think true love acted simple modesty.
               Come, night; come, Romeo; come, thou day in night,
               For thou wilt lie upon the wings of night
               Whiter than new snow on a raven's back.
               Come, gentle night, come, loving black-brow'd night,
               Give me my Romeo; and when he shall die,
               Take him and cut him out in little stars,
               And he will make the face of heaven so fine
               That all the world will be in love with night,
               And pay no worship to the garish sun.
               O, I have bought the mansion of a love,

But not possess'd it; and though I am sold,
Not yet enjoy'd. So tedious is this day
As is the night before some festival
To an impatient child that hath new robes,
And may not wear them.

Romeo and Juliet, III.ii.

COURTSHIP

Othello, a great Moorish general in the employ of the Venetian state, has abducted Desdemona, the daughter of Brabantio. Iago, Othello's batman, persuades Roderigo, who desires Desdemona, to rouse Brabantio in the middle of the night with the news. Shocked, the old man demands an immediate meeting of the Senate; Othello defends himself before them.

OTHELLO   This to hear
>Would Desdemona seriously incline;
>But still the house affairs would draw her thence;
>Which ever as she could with haste dispatch,
>She'd come again, and with a greedy ear
>Devour up my discourse. Which I observing,
>Took once a pliant hour, and found good means
>To draw her from a prayer of earnest heart
>That I would all my pilgrimage dilate
>Whereof by parcels she had something heard,
>But not intentively. I did consent,
>And often did beguile her of her tears,
>When I did speak of some distressful stroke
>That my youth suffer'd. My story being done,
>She gave me for my pains a world of sighs;
>She swore, in faith, 'twas strange, 'twas passing strange;
>'Twas pitiful, 'twas wondrous pitiful.
>She wish'd she had not heard it; yet she wish'd
>That heaven had made her such a man. She thank'd me;
>And bade me, if I had a friend that lov'd her,
>I should but teach him how to tell my story,
>And that would woo her. Upon this hint I spake;
>She lov'd me for the dangers I had pass'd,
>And I lov'd her that she did pity them.
>This only is the witchcraft I have us'd.

Othello, The Moor of Venice, I.iii.

FOLIE À DEUX

After the defeat of the conspirators who slew Julius Caesar, the Roman Empire is ruled by three men, M.Aemilius Lepidus ('a slight unmeritable man'), Octavius Caesar (Caesar's nephew) and Mark Antony. Antony has taken responsibility for the eastern Empire, including Egypt, and while there he has inevitably fallen to the charms of Cleopatra, Queen of Egypt. So potent is the passion between them that Antony prefers to stay by her side than go back to the centre of power, Rome. Octavius sends urgent missives demanding his immediate return. Antony ignores them.

ANTONY   Let Rome in Tiber melt, and the wide arch
                Of the rang'd empire fall! Here is my space.
                Kingdoms are clay; our dungy earth alike
                Feeds beast as man. The nobleness of life
                Is to do thus [*embracing*]; when such a mutual pair
                And such a twain can do't, in which I bind
                On pain of punishment, the world to weet
                We stand up peerless.

CLEOPATRA   Excellent falsehood!
                Why did he marry Fulvia, and not love her?
                I'll seem the fool I am not. Antony
                Will be himself.

ANTONY   But stirr'd by Cleopatra.
                Now for the love of Love and her soft hours,
                Let's not confound the time with conference harsh;
                There's not a minute of our lives should stretch
                Without some pleasure now. What sport to-night?

CLEOPATRA   Hear the ambassadors.

ANTONY   Fie, wrangling queen!
                    Whom everything becomes – to chide, to laugh,
                    To weep; whose every passion fully strives
                    To make itself, in thee fair and admir'd!
                    No messenger but thine, and all alone
                    To-night we'll wander through the streets and note
                    The qualities of people. Come my queen;
                    Last night you did desire it. Speak not to us.

                                        Antony and Cleopatra, I.i.

LOVE'S ECSTASY

As we have seen, Shakespeare's 154 sonnets chart an extraordinarily intense relationship between the poet and a beautiful and aristocratic young man, whose identity has been a source of debate since the poems were published in 1609. Starting lightly and pleasantly with a series of poems designed to encourage him to marry, they become more and more passionate, passing through jealousy to abject self-denigration, ending in uneasy farewell. This story is rendered somewhat opaque by the order in which the poems are printed (which may be deliberately scrambled); there are, in addition, twenty-seven poems addressed to the mistress. The collection adds up to one of the most remarkable accounts of love in the English language – or in any language. Here is a characteristically ecstatic meditation.

> What is your substance, whereof are you made,
> That millions of strange shadows on you tend?
> Since every one hath, every one, one shade,
> And you, but one, can every shadow lend?
> Describe Adonis, and the counterfeit
> Is poorly imitated after you;
> On Helen's cheek all art of beauty set,
> And you in Grecian tires are painted new.
> Speak of the spring and foison of the year:
> The one doth shadow of your beauty show,
> The other as your bounty doth appear,
> And you in every blessed shape we know.
>   In all external grace you have some part,
>   But you like none, none you, for constant heart.

Sonnet LIII

LOVE DAY AND NIGHT

One group of sonnets suggests that the poet has gone on a journey (perhaps to escape his fear that his mistress and his young friend will betray him with each other); as he travels, he stops for the night, but sleep eludes him because he is haunted by the vision of the friend's beauty.

When most I wink, then do mine eyes best see,
For all the day they view things unrespected;
But when I sleep, in dreams they look on thee,
And, darkly bright, are bright in dark directed.
Then thou whose shadow shadows doth make bright,
How would thy shadow's form form happy show
To the clear day with thy much clearer light,
When to unseeing eyes thy shade shines so!
How would, I say, mine eyes be blessed made
By looking on thee in the living day,
When in dead night thy fair imperfect shade
Through heavy sleep on sightless us doth stay!
  All days are night to see till I see thee,
  And nights bright days when dreams do show thee me.

Sonnet XLIII

ROYAL LOVE

$\mathcal{L}$ove is not necessarily any easier for monarchs than for their subjects – especially if they do not speak the same language. Henry V here woos Katherine of France in order to make a useful dynastic marriage. She is clearly not going to be steam-rollered into anything, however, and wittily uses the obstacles of grammar and vocabulary to make the passionate young soldier-king prove himself but the King stumbles on regardless in his enterprising Franglais.

KATHERINE Is it possible dat I sould love de enemy of France?

KING No, it is not possible you should love the enemy of France, Kate, but in loving me you should love the friend of France; for I love France so well that I will not part with a village of it; I will have it all mine. And, Kate, when France is mine and I am yours, then yours is France and you are mine.

KATHERINE I cannot tell vat is dat.

KING No, Kate? I will tell thee in French, which I am sure will hang upon my tongue like a new-married wife about her huband's neck, hardly to be shook off. Je quand sur le possession de France, et quand vous avez le possession de moi – let me see, what then? Saint Denis be my speed! – donc votre est France et vous êtes mienne. It is as easy for me, Kate, to conquer the kingdom as it is to speak so much more French: I shall never move thee in French, unless it be to laugh at me.

KATHERINE Sauf votre honneur, le Français que vous parlez, il est meilleur que l'Anglais lequel je parle.

KING   No faith, is't not, Kate; but thy speaking of my tongue, and I thine, most truly falsely, must needs be granted to be much at one. But, Kate, dost thou understand thus much English – Canst thou love me?

KATHERINE I cannot tell.

King Henry the Fifth, V.ii.

LOVE GONE WRONG

LOVE QUESTIONED
HAMLET

LOVE SPIED ON
HAMLET

LOVE REJECTED
HAMLET

MADNESS AND LOVE
HAMLET

LOVE'S AGONY
SONNET LVII

LOVE'S PARODY
KING RICHARD THE THIRD

JEALOUS LOVE
OTHELLO

LOVE QUESTIONED

*Ha*mlet, Prince of Denmark, tortured by his conviction that the death of his father, the late King, was brought about by foul play, has received powerful confirmation of this in his recent encounter with the old King's ghost. His behaviour becomes increasingly unpredictable. Ophelia is quizzed by her father, Polonius, on her relationship with the young Prince.

POLONIUS   What is between you? Give me up the truth.

OPHELIA   He hath, my lord, of late made many tenders
Of his affection to me.

POLONIUS   Affection! Pooh! You speak like a green girl,
Unsifted in such perilous circumstance.
Do you believe his tenders, as you call them?

OPHELIA   I do not know, my lord, what I should think.

POLONIUS   Marry, I'll teach you: think yourself a baby
That you have ta'en his tenders for true pay
Which are not sterling. Tender yourself more dearly;
Or – not to crack the wind of the poor phrase,
Running it thus – you'll tender me a fool.

OPHELIA   My lord, he hath importun'd me with love
In honourable fashion.

POLONIUS   Ay, fashion you may call it; go to, go to.

OPHELIA   And hath given countenance to his speech, my lord,
With almost all the holy vows of heaven.

POLONIUS   Ay, springes to catch woodcocks!

Hamlet, Prince of Denmark, I.iii.

LOVE SPIED ON

*W*ithout hesitation or conscience, Polonius forces his daughter to hand over a letter she has received from Hamlet, which only confirms for Polonius the instability of the young man's affections.

POLONIUS   I have a daughter – have while she is mine –
Who in her duty and obedience, mark,
Hath given me this. Now gather and surmise.   [*Reads*.

'To the celestial, and my soul's idol, the most beautified Ophelia.' That's an ill phrase, a vile phrase; 'beautified' is a vile phrase. But you shall hear. Thus: [*Reads*] 'In her excellent white bosom, these, etc.'

QUEEN   Came this from Hamlet to her?

POLONIUS   Good madam, stay awhile; I will be faithful. [*Reads*.

'Doubt thou the stars are fire;
Doubt that the sun doth move;
Doubt truth to be a liar;
But never doubt I love.

O dear Ophelia, I am ill at these numbers. I have not art to reckon my groans; but that I love thee best, O most best, believe it. Adieu.

Thine evermore, most dear lady, while this machine is to him,   HAMLET.'

This, in obedience, hath my daughter shown me; . . .

Hamlet, Prince of Denmark, II.ii.

LOVE REJECTED

*S*ecretly observed by Polonius and the usurping King, Hamlet's uncle Claudius, Hamlet has been meditating on suicide ('To be, or not to be'). Ophelia, primed by her father and the King, intercepts him with presents he has given her. He rejects them, then turns on her with frightening brutality.

HAMLET   If thou dost marry, I'll give thee this plague for thy dowry: be
            thou as chaste as ice, as pure as snow, thou shalt not escape
            calumny. Get thee to a nunnery, go, farewell. Or, if thou wilt
            needs marry, marry a fool; for wise men know well enough
            what monsters you make of them. To a nunnery, go; and
            quickly too. Farewell.

OPHELIA   O heavenly powers, restore him!

HAMLET   I have heard of your paintings too, well enough; God hath
            given you one face, and you make yourselves another. You jig
            and amble, and you lisp, and nickname God's creatures, and
            make your wantonness your ignorance. Go to, I'll no more
            on't; it hath made me mad. I say we will have no moe
            marriage: those that are married already, all but one,
            shall live; the rest shall keep as they are. To a nunnery, go.

Hamlet, Prince of Denmark, III.i.

MADNESS AND LOVE

The contradictory demands of love and filial duty, in conjunction with the violent death of her father, Polonius, at the hands of her sometime sweetheart, Hamlet, who has since been exiled to England, put more pressure on Ophelia's fragile mental equilibrium than it can bear. She erupts into the anxious court with flowers and herbs which she distributes to the King and Queen and her brother, Laertes, lately returned from abroad. Her thoughts, both in speech and in song, speak of terrible sexual confusion and distress.

OPHELIA   [*Sings*]   To-morrow is Saint Valentine's day,
                    All in the morning betime,
                    And I a maid at your window,
                    To be your Valentine.

                  Then up he rose, and donn'd his clothes,
                  And dupp'd the chamber door;
                  Let in the maid, that out a maid
                  Never departed more.

KING   Pretty Ophelia!

OPHELIA   Indeed, la, without an oath, I'll make an end on't.
        [*Sings*]   By Gis and by Saint Charity,
                    Alack, and fie for shame!
                  Young men will do't if they come to't;
                    By Cock, they are to blame.

                  Quoth she 'Before you tumbled me,
                    You promis'd me to wed.'

        He answers:
        'So would I 'a done, by yonder sun,
        An thou hadst not come to my bed.'

Hamlet, Prince of Denmark, IV.v.

LOVE'S AGONY

The lowest point of the Sonnets is reached with the poet feeling ignored
and unwanted by the friend he loves so desperately.

Being your slave, what should I do but tend
Upon the hours and times of your desire?
I have no precious time at all to spend,
Nor services to do, till you require;
Nor dare I chide the world-without-end hour,
Whilst I, my sovereign, watch the clock for you,
Nor think the bitterness of absence sour
When you have bid your servant once adieu;
Nor dare I question with my jealous thought
Where you may be, or your affairs suppose,
But, like a sad slave, stay and think of nought
Save where you are how happy you make those.
  So true a fool is love that in your will,
  Though you do anything, he thinks no ill.

Sonnet LVII

LOVE'S PARODY

— 🌹 —

𝒜ichard, Duke of Gloucester, having rid his brother, Edward IV, of the deposed and imprisoned Henry VI, sets his sights on the crown himself. Edward is ailing; Gloucester has plotted his brother George, Duke of Clarence's demise; the throne is within his sights. He needs a wife, though, and selects Lady Anne, widow of Edward, Prince of Wales, son of the late king, whom he helped to stab to death. 'What though I kill'd her husband and her father?/The readiest way to make the wench amends/Is to become her husband and her father'. He waylays her in the street as she accompanies her father-in-law's coffin, avowing his loving feelings for her.

ANNE	Black night o'ershade thy day, and death thy life!
GLOUCESTER	Curse not thyself, fair creature; thou art both.
ANNE	I would I were, to be reveng'd on thee.
GLOUCESTER	It is a quarrel most unnatural, To be reveng'd on him that loveth thee.
ANNE	It is a quarrel just and reasonable, To be reveng'd on him that killed my husband.
GLOUCESTER	He that bereft thee, lady, of thy husband Did it to help thee to a better husband.
ANNE	His better doth not breathe upon the earth.
GLOUCESTER	He lives that loves thee better than he could.
ANNE	Name him.
GLOUCESTER	Plantagenet.

ANNE	Why, that was he.
GLOUCESTER	The self-same name, but one of better nature.
ANNE	Where is he?
GLOUCESTER	Here. [*She spits at him*] Why dost thou spit at me?
ANNE	Would it were mortal poison, for thy sake!
GLOUCESTER	Never came poison from so sweet a place.

King Richard the Third, I.ii.

75

JEALOUS LOVE

Iago remorselessly, and with scientific precision, plots Othello's descent into homicidal jealousy. Othello, seen at the beginning of the play to have been profoundly in love with Desdemona, here, on the slenderest grounds, casts that love aside with careless impetuosity. Such are the fearful workings of jealousy.

IAGO Have you not sometimes seen a handkerchief
      Spotted with strawberries in your wife's hand?

OTHELLO I gave her such a one; 'twas my first gift.

IAGO I know not that, but such a handkerchief –
      I am sure it was your wife's – did I to-day
      See Cassio wipe his beard with.

OTHELLO   If it be that –

IAGO If it be that, or any that was hers,
      It speaks against her with the other proofs.

OTHELLO O that the slave had forty thousand lives!
      One is too poor, too weak for my revenge.
      Now do I see 'tis true. Look here, Iago –
      All my fond love thus do I blow to heaven.
      'Tis gone.
      Arise, black vengeance, from the hollow hell.
      Yield up, O love, thy crown and hearted throne
      To tyrannous hate! Swell bosom, with thy freight
      For 'tis of aspics' tongues.

IAGO   Yet be content.

OTHELLO   O, blood, blood, blood!

IAGO   Patience, I say; your mind perhaps may change.

OTHELLO   Never, Iago . . .

Othello, The Moor of Venice, III.iii.

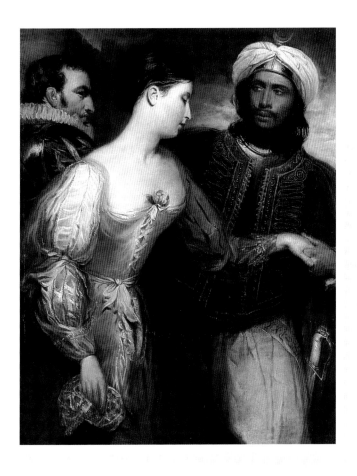

LOVE EMBRACED

LOVE REALISTIC
SONNET CXXX

SHREWD LOVE
SONNET CXXXVIII

SUBMISSIVE LOVE
THE TAMING OF THE SHREW

LOVE'S KINDNESS
SONNET CXXXXIII

MATURE LOVE
SONNET CIV

LOVE UNQUALIFIED
SONNET CXVI

TRANSCENDENT LOVE
SONNET XXXI

LOVE IN DEATH
ANTONY AND CLEOPATRA

LOVE REALISTIC

The poems in the collection of sonnets to Shakespeare's mistress are quite different in character from those addressed to the young man: here there is little sense of romantic infatuation; the feeling is entirely carnal, and there is a degree of realism about what love really is that is wholly absent from the highly charged outpourings of the other poems.

My mistress' eyes are nothing like the sun;
Coral is far more red then her lips' red;
If snow be white, why then her breasts are dun;
If hairs be wires, black wires grow on her head.
I have seen roses damask'd, red and white,
But no such roses see I in her cheeks;
And in some perfumes is there more delight
Than in the breath that from my mistress reeks.
I love to hear her speak, yet well I know
That music hath a far more pleasing sound;
I grant I never saw a goddess go –
My mistress when she walks treads on the ground.
  And yet, by heaven, I think my love as rare
  As any she belied by false compare.

Sonnet CXXX

SHREWD LOVE

Here, the poet wryly acknowledges the strategies that make love possible.

When my love swears that she is made of truth,
I do believe her though I know she lies,
That she might think me some untutor'd youth,
Unlearned in the world's false subtleties.
Thus vainly thinking that she thinks me young,
Although she knows my days are past the best,
Simply I credit her false-speaking tongue;
On both sides thus is simple truth suppress'd.
But wherefore says she not she is unjust,
And wherefore say not I that I am old?
O, love's best habit is in seeming trust,
And age in love loves not to have years told.
  Therefore I lie with her and she with me,
  And in our faults by lies we flattered be.

Sonnet CXXXVIII

SUBMISSIVE LOVE

In what is perhaps the least romantic of the plays, Shakespeare invites us to watch a strong-willed woman broken by a loutish man. Her subjugation is almost painful to watch, but the greatest actresses have been able to find in Kate's acceptance of her husband's dominance something complex, powerful and almost disturbing, as she mouths words that might have been written by her husband for her to say. Perhaps this is, after all, a kind of true love?

KATHARINE   Such duty as the subject owes the prince,
Even such a woman oweth to her husband;
And when she is froward, peevish, sullen, sour,
And not obedient to his honest will,
What is she but a foul contending rebel
And graceless traitor to her loving lord?
I am asham'd that women should be so simple
To offer war where they should kneel for peace;
Or seek for rule, supremacy, and sway,
When they are bound to serve, love, and obey.
Why are our bodies soft and weak and smooth,
Unapt to toil and trouble in the world,
But that our soft conditions and our hearts
Should well agree with our external parts?
Come, come you froward and unable worms!
My mind hath been as big as one of yours,
My heart as great, my reason haply more,
To bandy word for word and frown for frown;
But now I see our lances are but straws,
Our strength as weak, our weakness past compare,
That seeming to be most which we indeed least are.
Then vail your stomachs, for it is no boot,
And place your hands below your husband's foot;
In token of which duty, if he please,
My hand is ready, may it do him ease.

The Taming of the Shrew, V.ii.

LOVE'S KINDNESS

*A*nother from the sonnet sequence of 1609. After the torment of infidelity, the poet acknowledges that even though his mistress will continue to pursue her fancy, he needs and wants her comfort; interestingly, he compares her to a mother and himself to a neglected child.

> Lo as a careful huswife runs to catch
> One of her feathered creatures broke away,
> Sets down her babe, and makes all swift dispatch
> In pursuit of the thing she would have stay,
> Whilst her neglected child holds her in chase,
> Cries to catch her whose busy care is bent
> To follow that which flies before her face,
> Not prizing her poor infant's discontent;
> So runs't thou after that which flies from thee,
> Whilst I thy babe chase thee afar behind;
> But if thou catch thy hope, turn back to me,
> And play the mother's part, kiss me, be kind.
>   So will I pray that thou mayst have thy Will
>   If thou turn back and my loud crying still.

Sonnet CXXXXIII

MATURE LOVE

After the extremes of emotion endured by the poet in the course of his passionate engagement with the young man, or with the idea of the young man – which can be just as potent, just as painful – he reaches a calm and a security, confident now in his love. The only source of grief is the inevitability of time's ravages.

> To me, fair friend, you never can be old;
> For as you were when first your eye I ey'd,
> Such seems your beauty still. Three winters cold
> Have from the forests shook three summers' pride,
> Three beauteous springs to yellow autumn turn'd
> In process of the seasons have I seen,
> Three April perfumes in three hot Junes burn'd,
> Since first I saw you fresh, which yet art green.
> Ah, yet doth beauty, like a dial-hand,
> Steal from his figure and no pace perceiv'd;
> So your sweet hue, which methinks still doth stand,
> Hath motion, and mine eye may be deceiv'd.
>   For fear of which, hear this, thou age unbred:
>   Ere you were born was beauty's summer dead.

Sonnet CIV

LOVE UNQUALIFIED

— ❧ —

*W*hatever the tribulations of love, if it is true, the poet says, it will endure. When two people pledge themselves to each other, mere events and the depredations of time are powerless to destroy their love.

> Let me not to the marriage of true minds
> Admit impediments. Love is not love
> Which alters when it alteration finds,
> Or bends with the remover to remove.
> O, no! it is an ever-fixed mark,
> That looks on tempests and is never shaken;
> It's the star to every wand'ring bark,
> Whose worth's unknown, although his height be taken.
> Love's not Time's fool, though rosy lips and cheeks
> Within his bending sickle's compass come;
> Love alters not with his brief hours and weeks,
> But bears it out even to the edge of doom.
>   If this be error, and upon me prov'd,
>   I never writ, nor no man ever lov'd.

Sonnet CXVI

are the arms of certain knights of the round table
those that thus departed these are the chiefest. sir gaw

TRANSCENDENT LOVE

In an extraordinarily potent image, the poet finds that his present love
is not only richly rewarding in himself: he also contains within him all
the poet's past loves, so that, in loving him, the poet continues to love
all those others, who live again in him.

> Thy bosom is endeared with all hearts
> Which I by lacking have supposed dead;
> And there reigns love, and all love's loving parts,
> And all those friends which I thought buried.
> How many a holy and obsequious tear
> Hath dear religious love stol'n from mine eye
> As interest of the dead, which now appear
> But things remov'd that hidden in thee lie!
> Thou art the grave where buried love doth live,
> Hung with the trophies of my lovers gone,
> Who all their parts of me to thee did give;
> That due of many now is thine alone.
>   Their images I lov'd I view in thee,
>   And thou, all they, hast all the all of me.

Sonnet XXXI

LOVE IN DEATH

Antony has acknowledged the depth of his defeat at Caesar's hands, due largely to Cleopatra's indecisiveness. Cleopatra, terrified of his reproaches, has sent a messenger to say that she has killed herself. Antony determines on suicide, and asks his servant to kill him, but the boy kills himself instead. Antony falls on his own sword, but botches it, only to be told that Cleopatra was shamming. Dying, slowly and agonizingly, he is brought to her. He advises her how to behave when Caesar captures her, as he inevitably will. At first she refuses to believe that Antony is dying, but faced with the unavoidable truth, she rises to profound and simple eloquence.

CLEOPATRA   Noblest of men, woo't die?
        Hast no care of me? Shall I abide
        In this dull world, which in thy absence is
        No better than a sty? O, see my women,

                      [*Antony dies.*
        The crown o' th' earth doth melt. My lord!
        O, wither'd is the garland of the war,
        The soldier's pole is fall'n. Young boys and girls
        Are level now with men. The odds is gone,
        And there is nothing left remarkable
        Beneath the visiting moon.   [*Swoons.*

Antony and Cleopatra, IV.xv.

THE MANY FORMS OF LOVE

— ❧ —

LOVE OF A COMMANDER
ANTONY AND CLEOPATRA

LOVE FOR A MASTER
ANTONY AND CLEOPATRA

LOVE OF COUNTRY
KING RICHARD THE SECOND

LOVE OF KING
THE SECOND PART OF
KING HENRY THE FOURTH

LOVE OF A MENTOR
JULIUS CAESAR

BROTHERLY LOVE
HAMLET

LOVE DEMANDED
KING LEAR

FATHER/DAUGHTER LOVE
KING LEAR

LOVE OF CHILDREN
MACBETH

CANINE LOVE
THE TWO GENTLEMEN OF VERONA

LOVE ETERNAL
SONNET XVIII

LOVE OF A COMMANDER

℧he central figure of *Antony and Cleopatra* is Mark Antony, the pleasure-loving Roman general, enmeshed in an overwhelming sensuous relationship with the Egyptian Queen. Almost without exception, every character in the play loves Antony, even his opponents; yet one by one he disappoints them. Perhaps his most devoted companion is his lieutenant, Enobarbus, who nonetheless deserts him when he sees that Antony is bent on self-destruction. But Enobarbus's love of Antony is so great that he cannot live away from him; in this scene he simply dies from a broken heart, with Antony's name on his lips.

ENOBARBUS   O sovereign mistress of true melancholy,
                     The poisonous damp of night disponge upon me,
                     That life, a very rebel to my will,
                     May hang no longer on me. Throw my heart
                     Against the flint and hardness of my fault,
                     Which, being dried with grief, will break to powder,
                     And finish all foul faults. O Antony,
                     Nobler than my revolt is infamous,
                     Forgive me in thine own particular,
                     But let the world rank me in register
                     A master-leaver and a fugitive!
                     O Antony! O Antony!   [*Dies.*

Antony and Cleopatra, IV.ix.

LOVE FOR A MASTER

— ❀ —

Eros, one of Antony's faithful followers, is unable when the moment comes to follow through his promise to kill Antony. Instead he kills himself, the ultimate witness of the love he bears his master.

ANTONY   When I did make thee free, swor'st thou not then
              To do this when I bade thee? Do it at once,
              Or thy precedent services are all
              But accidents unpurpos'd. Draw, and come.

EROS   Turn from me then that noble countenance,
              Wherein the worship of the whole world lies.

ANTONY   Lo thee!   [*Turning from him.*

EROS   My sword is drawn.

ANTONY   Then let it do at once
              The thing why thou hast drawn it.

EROS   My dear master,
              My captain and my emperor, let me say,
              Before I strike this bloody stroke, farewell.

ANTONY   'Tis said, man; and farewell.

EROS   Farewell, great chief. Shall I strike now?

ANTONY   Now, Eros.

EROS   Why, there then! Thus do I escape the sorrow
              Of Antony's death.   [*Kills himself.*

ANTONY   Thrice nobler than myself!
Thou teachest me, O valiant Eros, what
I should, and thou couldst not. My queen and Eros
Have, by their brave instruction, got upon me
A nobleness in record. But I will be
A bridegroom in my death, and run into't
As to a lover's bed. Come then; and, Eros,
Thy master dies thy scholar . . . [*Falling on his sword.*

Antony and Cleopatra, IV.xiv

LOVE OF COUNTRY

John of Gaunt, Duke of Lancaster and the father of Henry Bolingbroke, is physically sick, but also sick at heart at what he conceives to be the ruin of his country at the hands of the feckless, narcissistic Richard II. On his deathbed, recounting England's past glory and present pride, he forsees a dire future for the country. In fact, after his death, his son was to usurp the throne, and, as Henry IV, to fight long and bitter battles for England's soul. Gaunt's passionate apostrophe to his native land has been a moving rallying cry for patriots ever since.

GAUNT   This royal throne of kings, this sceptr'd isle,
This earth of majesty, this seat of Mars,
This other Eden, demi-paradise,
This fortress built by Nature for herself
 Against infection and the hand of war,
This happy breed of men, this little world,
This precious stone set in the silver sea,
Which serves it in the office of a wall,
Or as a moat defensive to a house,
Against the envy of less happier lands;
This blessèd plot, this earth, this realm, this England,
This nurse, this teeming womb of royal kings,
Fear'd by their breed, and famous by their birth,

Renowned for their deeds as far from home,
For Christian service and true chivalry,
As is the sepulchre, in stubborn Jewry,
Of the world's ransom, blessed Mary's Son;
This land of such dear souls, this dear dear land,
Dear for her reputation through the world,
Is now leas'd out – I die pronouncing it –
Like to a tenement or pelting farm.

King Richard the Second, II.i.

LOVE OF KING

$\mathcal{E}$nshrined at the centre of Shakespeare's great historical epic is the unique relationship between the heir to the throne, John of Gaunt's grandson, Henry, Prince of Wales, or Hal, soon to be Henry V, and that magnificent reprobate, Sir John Falstaff. With his pendulous gut, his criminal ways and his wicked inversion of all conventional morality, he is as unlikely a companion to the future king as could be invented; yet Hal loves him, and his motley gang of henchmen love him, too, as do his mistress Doll Tearsheet and his landlady Mistress Quickly, hostess of the Boar's Head, to all of whom he has behaved disgracefully at one time or another. He exudes the irresistible life-force, and provides Hal with an opportunity both to understand life and to escape from the coldness of his upbringing. The time comes, however, when Hal has to take up his sword and show himself to be the hero the times call for. Finally, he assumes the crown. Falstaff rejoices; at last he will take his place at Hal's side. He rushes with his cronies to the coronation; alas, he is deceived. His time has passed. The most terrible words in all of Shakespeare are addressed to him: 'I know thee not, old man.' But until that moment he is confident in Hal's love of him.

FALSTAFF   Come here, Pistol; stand behind me. [*To Shallow*] O, if I had had time to have had made new liveries, I would have bestowed the thousand pound I borrowed of you. But 'tis no matter; this poor show doth better; this doth infer the zeal I had to see him.

SHALLOW   It doth so.

FALSTAFF   It shows my earnestness of affection –

SHALLOW   It doth so.

FALSTAFF   My devotion –

SHALLOW   It doth, it doth, it doth.

FALSTAFF As it were, to ride day and night; and not to deliberate, not
          to remember, not to have patience to shift me –
SHALLOW   It is best, certain.

FALSTAFF But to stand stained with travel, and sweating with desire to
          see him; thinking of nothing else, putting all affairs else in
          oblivion, as if there were nothing else to be done but to
          see him.

The Second Part of King Henry the Fourth, V.v.

LOVE OF A MENTOR

No sooner has Julius Caesar been killed than his favourite and surrogate son, Mark Antony, runs to the Capitol to confront his murderers. First begging them to kill him, he next embraces each in turn, then is suddenly caught short again by the sight of his patron and friend lying in a pool of blood.

ANTONY   That I did love thee, O, Caesar, 'tis true!
                 If then thy spirit look upon us now,
                 Shall it not grieve thee dearer than thy death
                 To see thy Antony making his peace,
                 Shaking the bloody fingers of thy foes,
                 Most noble! in the presence of thy corse?
                 Had I as many eyes as thou hast wounds,
                 Weeping as fast as they stream forth thy blood,
                 It would become me better than to close
                 In terms of friendship with thine enemies.
                 Pardon me, Julius! Here wast thou bay'd, brave hart;
                 Here didst thou fall; and here thy hunters stand,
                 Sign'd in thy spoil and crimson'd in thy lethe.
                 O world, thou wast the forest to this hart;
                 And this indeed, O world, the heart of thee!
                 How like a deer strucken by many princes
                 Dost thou here lie!

Julius Caesar, III.i.

BROTHERLY LOVE

*O*phelia drowns. Laertes, her brother, is shattered by her death, the more so for coming hot on the heels of Polonius's. Her funeral is a subdued affair; since she killed herself, she is not accorded a full Christian burial. Railing at the priest for his rigidness in the matter, Laertes is more and more overcome with wild grief, and finally jumps into the grave. Hamlet, who has just returned incognito from his exile, discovers for the first time that Ophelia is dead.

LAERTES   Lay her i' th' earth,
And from her fair and unpolluted flesh
May violets spring! I tell thee, churlish priest,
A minist'ring angel shall my sister be,
When thou liest howling.

HAMLET   What, the fair Ophelia!

QUEEN   Sweets to the sweet; farewell!
I hop'd thou shouldst have been my Hamlet's wife;
I thought thy bride-bed to have deck'd, sweet maid,
And not have strew'd thy grave.

LAERTES   O, treble woe
Fall ten times treble on that cursed head
Whose wicked deed thy most ingenious sense
Deprived thee of! Hold off the earth awhile,
Till I have caught her once more in mine arms.
        [Leaps into the grave.
Now pile your dust upon the quick and dead,
Till of this flat a mountain you have made
T' o'er-top old Pelion or the skyish head
Of blue Olympus.

Hamlet, Prince of Denmark, V.i.

LOVE DEMANDED

*L*ear, a king of ancient Britain, determines to divide up his kingdom among his three daughters. As he apportions the land, he demands to know how much each sister loves him. Regan and Goneril, his eldest, answer him in extravagant and fulsome terms; the youngest, Cordelia, hesitates.

LEAR   . . . what can you say to draw
                   A third more opulent than your sisters? Speak.

CORDELIA   Nothing, my lord.

LEAR   Nothing?

CORDELIA   Nothing.

LEAR   Nothing will come of nothing. Speak again.

CORDELIA   Unhappy that I am, I cannot heave
                   My heart into my mouth. I love your Majesty
                   According to my bond; no more, nor less.

LEAR   How, how, Cordelia! Mend your speech a little,
                   Lest you may mar your fortunes.

CORDELIA   Good my lord,
                   You have begot me, bred me, lov'd me; I
                   Return those duties back as are right fit,
                   Obey you, love you, and most honour you.
                   Why have my sisters husbands, if they say
                   They love you all? Haply, when I shall wed,
                   That lord whose hand must take my plight shall carry
                   Half my love with him, half my care and duty.
                   Sure I shall never marry like my sisters,
                   To love my father all.

LEAR   But goes thy heart with this?

CORDELIA   Ay, my good lord.

LEAR   So young and so untender?

CORDELIA   So young, my lord, and true.

LEAR   Let it be so! Thy truth, then, be thy dower!

King Lear, I.i.

FATHER/DAUGHTER LOVE

*R*egan and Goneril treat their father cruelly, refusing him his own retinue, finally allowing him to wander out on to the heath with his fool. There he meets up with the mad tramp, Poor Tom (who is in fact Edgar, the son of the Earl of Gloucester) and the disguised Earl of Kent, loyally following him to ensure his safety. But Lear's wits begin to desert him. On the cliffs of Dover he meets first the blinded Gloucester and then Cordelia, who the King of France has been fighting against the coalition of Regan and Goneril. She is infinitely moved to see her father again. Almost immediately the French are taken prisoner, and with them Lear and Cordelia, under the brutal command of Edmund, bastard son of Gloucester. Lear is unafraid, only happy to be with the daughter he loves.

CORDELIA   Shall we not see these daughters and these sisters?

LEAR   No, no, no, no! Come, let's away to prison.
We two alone will sing like birds i' th' cage;
When thou dost ask me blessing, I'll kneel down
And ask of thee forgiveness; so we'll live,
And pray, and sing, and tell old tales, and laugh
At gilded butterflies, and hear poor rogues
Talk of court news; and we'll talk with them too –
Who loses and who wins; who's in, who's out –
And take upon's the mystery of things
As if we were God's spies; and we'll wear out
In a wall'd prison packs and sects of great ones
That ebb and flow by th' moon.

EDMUND   Take them away.

LEAR   Upon such sacrifices, my Cordelia,
The gods themselves throw incense. Have I caught thee?
He that parts us shall bring a brand from heaven
And fire us hence like foxes. Wipe thine eyes;
The good years shall devour them, flesh and fell,
Ere they shall make us weep. We'll see 'em starved first.

King Lear, V.iii.

LOVE OF CHILDREN

General Macduff has deserted his former leader, Macbeth, the usurping King of Scotland, and made for England to make common cause with the self-exiled Malcolm, son of the murdered King Duncan, whom he seeks to persuade to take the leadership and crown of Scotland. Macduff is cheered to find Malcolm ready and willing, but is then immediately confronted by his cousin Ross with tragic news: his wife and children have been slaughtered by Macbeth's men.

MALCOLM   Merciful heaven!
What, man! Ne'er pull your hat upon your brows;
Give sorrow words. The grief that does not speak
Whispers the o'erfraught heart and bids it break.

MACDUFF   My children too?

ROSS   Wife, children, servants, all
That could be found.

MACDUFF   And I must be from thence!
My wife kill'd too?

ROSS   I have said.

MALCOLM   Be comforted.
Let's make med'cines of our great revenge
To cure this deadly grief.

MACDUFF   He has no children. All my pretty ones?
Did you say all? O hell-kite! All?
What, all my pretty chickens and their dam
At one fell swoop?

MALCOLM   Dispute it like a man.

MACDUFF   I shall do so;
            But I must also feel it as a man.
            I cannot but remember such things were
            That were most precious to me. Did heaven look on,
            And would not take their part? Sinful Macduff,
            They were all struck for thee – nought that I am;
            Not for their own demerits but for mine,
            Fell slaughter on their souls. Heaven rest them now!

                                        Macbeth, IV.iii.

CANINE LOVE

In *The Two Gentlemen of Verona,* Launce, the servant of Proteus, one of the gents of the title, is always accompanied by his dog, Crab. His love for the animal extends to taking his punishments for him. The speech proves not merely that human nature has changed very little since Shakespeare's time: canine nature remains pretty much the same too. Here Launce tells the audience something of Crab's criminal past.

LAUNCE   If I had not had more wit than he, to take a fault upon me that he did, I think verily he had been hang'd for't; sure as I live, he had suffer'd for't. You shall judge. He thrusts me himself into the company of three or four gentlemen-like dogs under the Duke's table; he had not been there, bless the mark, a pissing while but all the chamber smelt him. 'Out with the dog' says one; 'What cur is that?' says another; 'Whip him out' says the third; 'Hang him up' says the Duke. I, having been acquainted with the smell before, knew it was Crab, and goes me to the fellow that whips the dogs. 'Friend,' quoth I 'you mean to whip the dog.' 'Ay, marry do I' quoth he. 'You do him the more wrong,' quoth I ''twas I did the thing you wot of.' He makes me no more ado, but whips me out of the chamber. How many masters would do this for his servant?

The Two Gentlemen of Verona, IV.iv.

116

LOVE ETERNAL

One of the great themes of the Sonnets – eventually its dominant one – is that the sole way to brave time is through art, which renders both beauty and love immortal. In perhaps the most famous of all the Sonnets, the poet promises his young friend that his verse guarantees that the friend will live for ever: and, almost exactly 400 years later, he and it are still alive for us.

Shall I compare thee to a summer's day?
Thou art more lovely and more temperate.
Rough winds do shake the darling buds of May,
And summer's lease hath all too short a date:
Sometime too hot the eye of heaven shines,
And often is his gold complexion dimm'd;
Every fair from fair sometime declines,
By chance, or nature's course untrimm'd;
But thy eternal summer shall not fade
Nor lose possession of that fair thou ow'st;
Nor shall Death brag thou wand'rest in his shade,
When in eternal lines to time thou grow'st.
  So long as men can breathe or eyes can see,
  So long lives this, and this gives life to thee.

Sonnet XVIII

INDEX OF ARTISTS AND PAINTINGS

TITLE PAGE
'Ideal' Portrait of William Shakespeare
detail
Angelica Kauffman (1741-1807)
Royal Shakespeare Company

PAGE 6-7
Early 18th-century fresco *detail*
Giuseppe Fontebasso
Venice

PAGE 9
The Globe Theatre
George Shepherd (1800-1830)
The British Museum, London

PAGE 12-13
The Rural Concert *detail*
Giorgione (active 1506; died 1510)
Louvre, Paris

PAGE 15
Rosalind and Celia as Ganymede and
Aliena in the Forest of Arden *detail*
Walter Howell Deverell (1827-1854)
Shipley Art Gallery, Gateshead

PAGE 16
Musical Angel *detail*
Rosso Fiorentino (1494-1540)
Galleria degli Uffizi, Florence

PAGE 19
Portrait of a Young Man *detail*
Andrea del Sarto (1486-1530)
The National Gallery, London

PAGE 20-21
Miranda - 'The Tempest'
John William Waterhouse (1849-191
Private Collection

PAGE 23
Rosalind in the Forest *detail*
Sir John Everett Millais (1829-1896
Walker Art Gallery, Liverpool

PAGE 25
The Hireling Shepherd *detail*
William Holman Hunt (1827-1910)
The Makins Collection, Washington, D.C.

PAGE 26-27
Thomas King as Touchstone in
'As You Like It'
Johann Zoffany (1733-1810)
The Garrick Club, London

PAGE 28-29
The Awakening of Adonis *detail*
ohn **William Waterhouse** (1849-1917)
Private Collection

PAGE 31
Portrait of a Girl
Workshop of Domenico Ghirlandaio
(probably about 1490)
The National Gallery, London

PAGE 32
Romeo and Juliet *detail*
Sir Frank Dicksee (1853-1928)
Southampton City Art Gallery, Hampshire

PAGE 34
'The Taming of the Shrew':
Katherine and Petruchio
Robert Braithwaite Martineau
(1826-1869)
Ashmolean Museum, Oxford

PAGE 37
Ariel
Henry Fuseli (1741-1825)
Folger Shakespeare Library, Washington, D.C.

PAGE 39
Titania and Bottom
Henry Fuseli (1741-1825)
Tate Gallery, London

PAGE 41
Scenes from 'As You Like It' *detail*
Arthur Hughes (1832-1915)
Walker Art Gallery, Liverpool

PAGE 43
Venus and Adonis *detail*
Jacopo Amigoni (about 1682-1752)
Private Collection

PAGE 44-45
Dame Edith Evans and Sir Godfrey Tearle
as Antony in 'Antony and Cleopatra' *detail*
Felix Topolski (1907-1989)
The Garrick Club, London

PAGE 46
Claudio and Isabella *detail*
William Holman Hunt (1827-1910)
Tate Gallery, London

PAGE 49
'Twelfth Night', Act II, Scene 3
Eduard Grutzner (1846-1925)
Private Collection

PAGE 51
The Crown of Love
Sir John Everett Millais (1829-1896)
Private Collection

PAGE 52
Othello and Desdemona in Venice *detail*
Théodore Chassériau (1819-1856)
Louvre, Paris

PAGE 55
Anthony and Cleopatra
Gerbrandt van den Eeckhout (1621-1674)
Johannesburg Art Gallery, South Africa

PAGE 57
Paul Scofield in 'The Winter's Tale' *detail*
Dame Laura Knight (1877-1970)
Royal Shakespeare Company

PAGE 65
Ophelia and Laertes *detail*
William Gordon Wills (1828-1891)
Private Collection

PAGE 59
'Romeo and Juliet', Act V, Scene 2 *detail*
Ferdinand Piloty (1828-1895)
Royal Shakespeare Company

PAGE 61
Lewis Waller as Henry V
Arthur Hacker (1858-1919)
Royal Shakespeare Company

PAGE 62-63
Ophelia *detail*
Sir John Everett Millais (1829-1896)
Tate Gallery, London

PAGE 66
The Pained Heart, or
'Sigh no More, Ladies' *detail*?
Arthur Hughes (1832-1915)
Private Collection

PAGE 75
Sir John Martin-Harvey as Richard III
detail
Bernard Munns (1870-1942)
Royal Shakespeare Company

PAGE 80
Gypsy Girl
Frans Hals (about 1580-1666)
Louvre, Paris

PAGE 69
Edwin Booth as Hamlet
Oliver Ingraham Lay (1845-1890)
Royal Shakespeare Company

PAGE 77
Othello, Desdemona and Iago
Henry Munro (1791-1814)
Private Collection

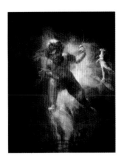

PAGE 83
Puck
Henry Fuseli (1741-1825)
Folger Shakespeare Library, Washington, D.C.

PAGE 70
Ophelia *detail*
Ferdinand Piloty (1828-1895)
Royal Shakespeare Company

PAGE 78-79
The Reconciliation of the Montagues
and Capulets *detail*
Frederic, Lord Leighton (1830-1896)
Agnes Scott College, Decatur, Georgia

PAGE 84
Miss Ada Rehan as Katharine *detail*
Eliot Gregory (1854-1915)
Royal Shakespeare Company

PAGE 72
Portrait of a Man *detail*
Francesco Franciabigio
(about 1482-1525)
Louvre, Paris

PAGE 87
St.Peter Distributes Alms, and the
Death of Ananias *detail*
Masaccio (1401-probably 1428)
*S. Maria del Carmine, Brancacci Chapel,
Florence*

PAGE 88
The Man with the Glove
Titian (active about 1506; died 1576)
Louvre, Paris

PAGE 90-91
Painter's Honeymoon *detail*
Frederic, Lord Leighton (1830-1896)
Museum of Fine Arts, Boston

PAGE 92-93
Verdure with Deer and Shields
(tapestry detail)
Designed by Sir Edward Burne-Jones
(1833-1898)
Birmingham Museums and Art Gallery

PAGE 94
The Death of Antony and Cleopatra
detail
Alessandro Turchi (1579-1649)
Louvre, Paris

PAGE 96-97
Young Man Beside the Sea *detail*
Hippolyte Flandrin (1809-1864)
Louvre, Paris

PAGE 99
General Bonaparte on the Bridge at Arcola
detail
Baron Antoine-Jean Gros (1771-1835)
Château de Versailles, Paris

PAGE 101
Warrior with Shield Bearer
Giorgione (active 1506; died 1510)
Galleria degli Uffizi, Florence

PAGE 102-103
Shakespeare's Cliff
David Cox (1783-1859)
Private Collection

PAGE 105
Portrait of Sir Ralph Richardson
as Falstaff
Ruskin Spear (1911-1990)
The National Theatre, London

PAGE 106
The Death of the Rebel, Viriathus *detail*
Raimundo de Madrazo y Garetta
(1841-1920)
Prado, Madrid

PAGE 109
Mr Glen Byam Shaw as Laertes *detail*
Glyn Philpot (1904-1986)
Royal Shakespeare Company

PAGE 113
Juliet and Friar Lawrence
John Pettie (1839-1893)
Royal Shakespeare Company

PAGE 117
A Terrier *detail*
John Fitz Marshall (1859-1932)
Private Collection

PAGE 111
King Lear and his Three Daughters
William Hilton (1786-1839)
Private Collection

PAGE 115
The Massacre of the Innocents *detail*
Pieter Bruegel the Elder
(active 1550/1; died 1569)
Kunsthistorisches Museum, Vienna

PAGE 118
Dame Alice Ellen Terry (Choosing)
George Frederic Watts (1817-1904)
The National Portrait Gallery, London

PHOTOGRAPHIC ACKNOWLEDGMENTS

The Publishers have made every effort to contact all holders of copyright works. All copyright-holders we have been unable to reach are invited to contact the Publishers so that a full acknowledgment may be given in subsequent editions. For permission to reproduce the paintings on the following pages and for supplying photographs, the Publishers thank:

Agnes Scott College, Decatur, Georgia 78-79; **AKG London** 16, 88; **AKG London/Erich Lessing** 12-13, 52, 80, 87, 96-97, 115; **Bridgeman Art Library** 25, 32, 34, 43 (Agnew & Sons), 55, 66 (The Maas Gallery), 92-93, 101, 105 (© Courtesy of the artist's estate), 106, 117 (Christopher Wood Gallery, London); **The British Museum, London/E.T. Archive** 9; **Christie's Images/Bridgeman Art Library** 49; © **Christie's Images Ltd 1999** 28-29; **E.T. Archive** 102-103; **Fine Art Photographic Library Ltd** 51; **By permission of the Folger Shakespeare Library** 37, 83; **The Garrick Club, London/E.T. Archive** 26-27, 44-45; **Giraudon/Bridgeman Art Library** 94, 99; **Courtesy, Museum of Fine Arts, Boston** (Charles H. Bayley Picture and Painting Fund, 1981.258) 90-91; © **National Gallery, London** 19, 31; **Board of Trustees of the National Museums and Galleries on Merseyside** (Walker Art Gallery) 23, 41; **By courtesy of the National Portrait Gallery, London** 118; © **photo RMN – Gérard Blot** 72; **From the RSC Collection with the permission of the Governors of the Royal Shakespeare Theatre** Title page, 57, 59, 61, 69, 70, 75, 84, 109 (painting on loan), 113; **Shipley Art Gallery (Tyne and Wear Museums)** 15; **Sotheby's Picture Library** 20-21, 65, 77, 111; **Tate Gallery, London** 46, 62-63; **Tate Gallery, London/E.T. Archive** 39; © **Simon Upton** 6-7